WOMEN
IN THE
CIVIL WAR

Warriors, Patriots, Nurses, and Spies

PHYLLIS RAYBIN EMERT

 Perspectives on History

D1225997

**History**Compass

Boston, Massachusetts

HistoryCompass
www.historycompass.com

ISBN 978-1-932663-19-8 paperback edition

Printed in the United States of America

Photo/Illustration Credits:

"Harriet Tubman" (p. 22), "Belle Boyd" (p. 33), "Rose O'Neal Greenhow and daughter" (p. 43). Courtesy: Library of Congress. "Louisa May Alcott" (p. 55). Courtesy: The Louisa May Alcott Memorial Association.

Library of Congress Cataloging-in-Publication Data
Women in the Civil War: warriors, patriots, nurses, and spies /
edited by Phyllis Raybin Emert. — 2nd ed. p. cm.
Includes bibliographical references and index.
ISBN-13: 978-1-932663-19-8 (alk. paper)

1. United States--History – Civil War, 1861-1865--Women.
2. United States--History – Civil War, 1861-1865 – Women--Sources.
3. United States--History – Civil War, 1861-1865 – Personal narratives.
4. United States--History – Civil War, 1861-1865 – Biography.
5. Women--United States--Biography. I. Emert, Phyllis Raybin.
 E628.W66 2007
 973.7'4 – dc22
 2007028393

Table of Contents

Dedication
For Melissa Emert

Foreword

Many believe that the Civil War was the greatest single event in United States history. More than 600,000 Americans lost their lives in this conflict between the North and the South.

Women in the Civil War focuses on the roles women played, their influence, contributions, and first-hand experiences from 1861 through 1865.

The women in this book contributed to their respective causes in various ways. Some used written words to influence people, while others relied on the spoken word to sway opinion.

Some risked their lives as spies and soldiers to gather valuable information for their cause. Many volunteered to help wounded and sick soldiers in military hospitals throughout the North and South, jeopardizing their own health in the process.

Still other women kept journals and diaries (and many interviews were conducted and recorded) that give the readers of today a glimpse of what life was like for women at all levels of society during the Civil War years.

This book focuses on female activists during a significant period in United States history, using their own words, thoughts, and opinions. It is divided into four major sections: Freedom Fighters, Spies and Secrets, Supporting the Troops, and On the Homefront.

Harriet Beecher Stowe

By the mid-19th century, America was deeply divided on the issue of slavery. Both the North and the South were concerned with whether new territories would enter the Union as slave or free states.

It was the passage of the Fugitive Slave Act in 1850 which moved author Harriet Beecher Stowe to finally write about the subject of slavery. This law punished anyone who helped slaves to escape. If caught, fugitives were not allowed a jury trial, could not testify on their behalf, and were almost always returned to their often brutal masters.

As opposition to slavery increased in the North, Stowe declared, "Up to this year I have always felt that I had no particular call to meddle with this subject.... But I feel now that the time is come when even a woman or a child who can speak a word for freedom and humanity is bound to speak."

First published in weekly installments in the National Era newspaper, and then in book form in 1852, Uncle Tom's Cabin sold 300,000 copies in one year. To date, millions of copies have been published in different languages throughout the world.

Stowe's book stirred the nation's conscience and its impact could be felt in the atmosphere that helped bring about the Civil War. An excerpt from Uncle Tom's Cabin follows:

> The child, a boy of ten months, was uncommonly large and strong of his age, and very vigorous in his

limbs. Never, for a moment, still, he kept his mother constantly busy in holding him, and guarding his springing activity.

"That's a fine chap!" said a man, suddenly stopping opposite to him, with his hands in his pockets. "How old is he?"

"Ten months and a half," said the mother.

The man whistled to the boy and offered him part of a stick of candy, which he eagerly grabbed at, and very soon had it in a baby's general depository, to wit, his mouth.

"Rum fellow!" said the man. "Knows what's what!" and he whistled, and walked on. When he had got to the other side of the boat, he came across Haley, who was smoking on top of a pile of boxes....

"Taking her down south?" said the man.

Haley nodded and smoked on....

"They won't want the young 'un on the plantation," said the man.

"I shall sell him, first chance I find," said Haley, lighting another cigar....

"Well, stranger, what will you take?"

"Well now," said Haley, "I *could* raise that ar chap myself, or get him raised; he's uncommon likely and healthy, and he'd fetch a hundred dollars, six months hence; and, in a year or two, he'd bring two hundred, if I had him in the right spot;—so I shan't take a cent less nor fifty for him now."

"O, stranger! that's rediculous, altogether," said the man.

"Fact!" said Haley, with a decisive nod of his head.

"I'll give thirty for him," said the stranger, "but not a cent more."

"Now, I'll tell ye what I will do," said Haley, spitting again, with renewed decision. "I'll split the difference, and say forty-five, and that's the most I will do."

"Well, agreed!" said the man, after an interval.

"Done!" said Haley. "Where do you land?"

"At Louisville," said the man.

"Louisville," said Haley. "Very fair, we get there about dusk. Chap will be asleep,—all fair,—get him off quietly, and no screaming,—happens beautiful,—I like to do everything quietly,—I hates all kind of agitation and fluster." And so, after a transfer of certain bills had passed from the man's pocket-book to the trader's he resumed his cigar.

It was a bright, tranquil evening when the boat stopped at the wharf at Louisville. The woman had been sitting with her baby in her arms, now wrapped in a heavy sleep. When she heard the name of the place called out, she hastily laid the child down in a little cradle formed by the hollow among the boxes, first carefully spreading under it her cloak; and then she sprung to the side of the boat, in hopes that, among the various hotel-waiters who thronged the wharf, she might see her husband. In this hope, she pressed forward to the front rails, and, stretching far over them, strained her eyes intently on the moving heads on the shore, and the crowd pressed in between her and the child.

"Now's your time," said Haley, taking the sleeping child up, and handing him to the stranger. "Don't wake him up, and set him to crying, now; it would make a devil of a fuss with the gal." The man took the bundle carefully, and was soon lost in the crowd that went up the wharf.

When the boat, creaking, and groaning, and puffing, had loosed from the wharf, and was beginning slowly to strain herself along, the woman returned to her old seat. The trader was sitting there,—the child was gone!

"Why, why,—where?" she began, in bewildered surprise.

"Lucy," said the trader, "Your child's gone; you may as well know it first as last. You see, I know'd you couldn't take him down south; and I got a chance to sell him to a first-rate family, that'll raise him better than you can."...

...The wild look of anguish and utter despair that the woman cast on him might have disturbed one less practiced; but he was used to it. He had seen that same look hundreds of times. You can get used to such things, too, my friend; and it is the great object of recent efforts to make our whole northern community used to them, for the glory of the Union. So the trader only regarded the mortal anguish which he saw working in those dark features, those clenched hands, and suffocating breathings, as necessary incidents of the trade, and merely calculated whether she was going to scream, and get up a commotion on the boat; for, like other supporters of our peculiar institution, he decidedly disliked agitation.

But the woman did not scream. The shot had passed too straight and direct through the heart, for cry or tear.

Dizzily she sat down. Her slack hands fell lifeless by her side. Her eyes looked straight forward, but she saw nothing. All the noise and hum of the boat, the groaning of the machinery, mingled dreamily to her bewildered ear; and the poor, dumb-stricken heart had neither cry not tear to show for its utter misery. She was quite calm....

Tom drew near, and tried to say something; but she only groaned. Honestly, and with tears running down his own cheeks, he spoke of a heart of love in the skies, of a pitying Jesus, and an eternal home; but the ear was deaf with anguish, and the palsied heart could not feel.

Night came on,—night calm, unmoved, and glorious, shining down with her innumerable and solemn angel eyes, twinkling, beautiful, but silent. There was no speech nor language, no pitying voice or helping hand, from that distant sky. One after another, the voices of business or pleasure died away; all on the boat were sleeping, and the ripples at the prow were plainly heard. Tom stretched himself out on a box, and there, as he lay, he heard, ever and anon, a smothered sob or cry from the prostrate creature,—"O! what shall I do? O Lord! O good Lord, do help me!" and so, ever and anon, until the murmur died away in silence.

At midnight, Tom waked, with a sudden start. Something black passed quickly by him to the side of the boat, and he heard a splash in the water. No one else saw or heard anything. He raised his head,—the woman's place was vacant! He got up, and sought about him in vain. The poor bleeding heart was still, at last, and the river rippled and dimpled just as brightly as if it had not closed above it....

The trader waked up bright and early, and came out to see to his live-stock. It was now his turn to look about in perplexity.

Where alive is that gal?" he said to Tom....

"Well, Mas'r," said Tom, "towards morning something brushed by me, and I kinder half woke; and then I hearn a great splash, and then I clare woke up, and the gal was gone. That's all I know on 't."

The trader was not shocked nor amazed; because, as we said before, he was used to a great many things that you are not used to. Even the awful presence of Death struck no solemn chill upon him. He had seen Death many times,—met him in the way of trade, and got acquainted with him,—and he only thought of him as a hard customer, that embarrassed his property operations very unfairly; and so he only swore that the gal was a baggage, and that he was devilish unlucky, and that, if things went on in this way, he should not make a cent on the trip. In short, he seemed to consider himself an ill-used man, decidedly; but there was no help for it, as the woman had escaped into a state which *never will* give up a fugitive,—not even at the demand of the whole glorious Union. The trader, therefore, sat discontentedly down, with his little account-book, and put down the missing body and soul under the head of *losses!*

Source: Harriet Beecher Stowe, *Uncle Tom's Cabin* (New York: New American Library, 1998), pp. 139-45.

Sojourner Truth Speaks Out

She was a freed slave, born and raised in New York and with Dutch as her native language, who once was called Isabella. After renaming herself Sojourner Truth, she became an outspoken orator in her fight against slavery, as well as in support of women's rights. Although she never learned to read or write, her speeches throughout the country often moved her audiences to tears.

When Truth addressed a women's rights convention in 1851, she was met at first with jeers and boos from the men in the crowd. An excerpt from that address, as recorded by an observer in Truth's Narrative, *is as follows:*

"Well, chilern, whar dar is so much racket dar must be something out o' kilter. I tink dat 'twixt de niggers of de Souf and de women at de Norf all a talkin' 'bout rights, de white men will be in a fix pretty soon. But what's all dis here talkin' 'bout? Dat man ober dar say dat women needs to be helped into carriages, and lifted ober ditches, and to have de best place every whar. Nobody eber help me into carriages, or ober mud puddles, or gives me any best place [and raising herself to her full hight [sic] and her voice to a pitch like rolling thunder, she asked], and ar'n't I a woman?...I have borne thirteen chilern and seen 'em mos' all sold off into slavery, and when I cried out with a mother's grief, none but Jesus heard—and ar'n't I a woman?"

Source: Nell Irvin Painter, ed., *Narrative of Sojourner Truth* (New York: Penguin Books, 1998), p. 92.

Before her speeches, Sojourner Truth often sang anti-slavery hymns which she made up herself, an example of which follows:

I am pleading for my people—
A poor downtrodden race,
Who dwell in freedom's boasted land,
With no abiding place.

I am pleading that my people
May have their rights astored [restored]
For they have long been toiling,
And yet had no reward....

Whilst I bear upon my body
the scars of many a gash,
I am pleading for my people
Who groan beneath the lash....

I plead with you to sympathize
With sighs and groans and scars,
And note how base the tyranny
Beneath the stripes and stars.

Source: Painter, p. 208.

When the Civil War began in 1861, Sojourner Truth was already in her sixties. She was an active supporter of President Abraham Lincoln and believed he was a good friend to blacks everywhere.

In 1864, Truth traveled to Washington from her home in Battle Creek, Michigan, and met privately with Abraham Lincoln. Her account of the meeting follows:

It was about 8 o'clock A.M., when I called on the president. Upon entering his reception room we found about a dozen persons in waiting, among them two colored women. I had quite a pleasant time waiting until he was disengaged, and enjoyed his conversation with others; he showed as much kindness and consideration to the colored persons as to the whites—if there was any difference, more....

The president was seated at his desk. Mrs. C. said to him, "This is Sojourner Truth, who has come all the way from Michigan to see you." He then arose, gave me his hand, made a bow, and said, "I am pleased to see you."

I said to him, Mr. President, when you first took your seat I feared you would be torn to pieces, for I likened you unto Daniel, who was thrown into the lion's den; and if the lions did not tear you into pieces, I knew that it would be God that had saved you; and I said if he spared me I would see you before the four years expired, and he has done so, and now I am here to see you for myself....

I must say, and I am proud to say, that I never was treated by anyone with more kindness and cordiality
than were shown to me by that great and good man, Abraham Lincoln....He took my little book, and with the same hand that signed the death-warrant of slavery, he wrote as follows:

"For Aunty Sojourner Truth,

Oct. 29, 1864.

A. Lincoln."

Source: Painter, pp. 120-21.

Charlotte Forten

Free, black, and educated, Charlotte Forten grew up in Massachusetts in a family which was actively involved in the anti-slavery movement. The 17-year-old Charlotte wrote the following words in her journal in September 1855:

... let us labor earnestly and faithfully to acquire knowledge, to break down the barriers of prejudice and oppression. Let us take courage; never ceasing to work,—hoping and believing that if not for us, for another generation there is a better, brighter day in store, when slavery and prejudice shall vanish before the glorious light of Liberty and Truth; when the rights of every colored man shall everywhere be acknowledged and respected, and he shall be treated as a *man* and a *brother*.

Source: Brenda Stevenson, ed., *The Journals of Charlotte Forten Grimke* (New York: Oxford University Press, 1988), p. 140.

During the Civil War, Union forces captured the South Carolina Sea Islands and Port Royal area in late 1861. There they found 10,000 slaves who had been deserted by their Confederate masters. These slaves were very poor, could not read or write, and spoke a garbled speech which was difficult to understand.

Port Royal became the scene of a great social experiment to allow these freed slaves a chance to prove themselves, and abolition societies in New York, Boston, and Philadelphia donated money to pay the salaries of volunteer teachers to travel to Port Royal to teach the newly freed people. In 1862, 24-year-old Charlotte Forten was one of more than fifty volunteers and the only black person among them. Forten recorded her detailed experiences at Port Royal in her journal from October 1862 to May 1864, as set forth in the following excerpts:

Tuesday Night [October 28, 1862]. Went into the Commissary's Office to wait for the boat which was to take us to St. Helena's Island which is about six miles from B.[eaufort]. Tis here that Miss [Laura] Towne has her school, in which I am to teach....While waiting in the office we saw several military gentleman [sic], *not* very creditable specimens, I sh'ld say. The little Commissary himself, Capt. T. is a perfect little popinjay, and he and a Colonel somebody who didn't look any too sensible, talked in a very smart manner, evidently for our especial benefit. The word "nigger" was plentifully used, whereupon I set them down at once as *not* gentleman [sic]. Then they talked a great deal about rebel attacks and yellow fever, and other alarming things, with significant nods and looks at each other. We saw through them at once, and were not at all alarmed by any of their representations. But if they are a fair example of army officers, I sh'ld pray to see as little of them as possible.

Wednesday, Oct. 29.... We went into the school, and heard the children read and spell. The teachers tell us that they have made great improvement in a very short time, and I noticed with pleasure how bright, how eager to learn many of them seem. The singing delighted me most. They sang beautifully in their rich, sweet clear tones, and with that peculiar swaying motion which I had noticed before in the older people, and which seems to make their singing all the more effective....Dear children! born in slavery, but free at last? May God preserve to you all the blessings of freedom, and may you be in every possible way fitted to enjoy them. My heart goes out to you. I shall be glad to do all that I can to help you.—

Wednesday, November 5.... Part of my scholars are very tiny,—babies, I call them—and it is hard to keep them quiet and interested while I am hearing the larger ones. They are too young even for the alphabet, it seems to me. I think I must write home and ask somebody to send me picture-books and toys to amuse them with....

Thursday, November 13.... Talked to the children a little while to-day about the noble [Haitian revolutionary leader] Toussaint. They listened very attentively. It is well that they sh'ld know what one of their own color c'ld do for his race. I long to inspire them with courage and ambition (of a noble sort), and high purpose....

Source: Stevenson, pp. 389, 391, 394, 397-98.

Forten also wrote about her experiences in an article in the Atlantic Monthly, *excerpts from which follow:*

The first day of school was rather trying. Most of my children were very small, and consequently restless....These little ones were brought to school because the older children—in whose care their parents leave them while at work—could not come without them. We were therefore willing to have them come, although they seemed to have discovered the secret of perpetual motion, and tried one's patience sadly....I never before saw children so eager to learn, although I had had several years' experience in New-England schools. Coming to school is a constant delight and recreation to them. They come here as other children go to play. The older ones, during the summer, work in the fields from early morning until eleven or twelve o'clock, and then come into school, after their hard toil in the hot sun, as bright and as anxious to learn as ever.

...Many of the grown people are desirous of learning to read. It is wonderful how a people who have been so long crushed to the earth, so imbruted as these have been,—and they are said to be among the most degraded negroes of the South,—can have so great a desire for knowledge, and such a capability for attaining it. One cannot believe that the haughty Anglo-Saxon race, after centuries of such an experience as these people have had, would be very much superior to them. And one's indignation increases against those who, North as well as South, taunt the colored race with inferiority while they themselves use every means in their power to crush and degrade them, denying them every right and privilege, closing against them every avenue of elevation and improvement....

Source: Charlotte Forten, "Life on the Sea Islands," *Atlantic Monthly*, 13 (May and June 1864), *reprinted in* Louis P. Masur, *The Real War Will Never Get in the Books* (New York: Oxford University Press, 1993), p. 156.

Harriet Tubman

Born a slave in Dorchester County, Maryland, Harriet Tubman escaped to the north in 1849 and became involved in the abolitionist movement. The ex-slave returned secretly to the south again and again to help as many of her people escape from slavery as she could. Called the "Moses" of her people, Tubman risked her own life time after time, and led small groups of fugitive slaves north on the Underground Railroad. This was the term given to a secret group of people who offered food, shelter, and a place to hide to those seeking their freedom. Traveling by night and hidden by day, Tubman managed to lead more than 300 slaves out of bondage. Although only five feet tall, Tubman was a very strong woman who had once worked as a field hand. According to Agatha Young in The Women and the Crisis, *"Sometimes the fatigue, the hunger and the fear would be too much for one or another of the slaves to bear, but Tubman would let no one turn back for fear the rest would*

Harriet Tubman.

be discovered. She carried a revolver and if one of them, exhausted, refused to go further, she took it out and aimed it at him, saying, 'Dead niggers tell no tales. You go on or die.'" (Agatha Young, The Women and the Crisis *(New York: McDowell, Obolensky, 1959), p. 300.)*

Harriet Tubman once said, "On my underground railroad I nebber run my train off de track an' I nebber los' a passenger." This quote is inscribed on a tablet placed in her memory at the front entrance of the courthouse in Auburn, New York.

Charlotte Forten wrote of a meeting with Harriet Tubman in her journal while they were both volunteers at Port Royal, South Carolina in 1863, as follows:

In B. [eaufort] we spent nearly all our time at Harriet Tubman's otherwise [known as] "Moses." She is a wonderful woman—a real heroine. Has helped off a large number of slaves, after taking her own freedom. She told us that she used to hide them in the woods during the day and go around to get provisions for them. Once she had with her a man named Joe, for whom a reward of $1500 was offered. Frequently, in different places she found handbills exactly describing him, but at last they reached in safety the Suspension Bridge over the Falls and found themselves in Canada. Until then, she said, Joe had been very silent. In vain had she called his attention to

---

the glory of the Falls. He sat perfectly still—moody, it seemed, and w'ld not even glance at them. But when she said, "Now we are in Can.[ada]" he sprang to his feet—with a great shout and sang and clapped his hands in a perfect delirium of joy. So when they got out, and he first touched *free* soil, he shouted and hurrahed "as if he were crazy"—she said. How exciting it was to hear her tell the story. And to hear her sing the very scraps of jubilant hymns that he sang. She said the ladies crowded around them, and some laughed and some cried. My own eyes were full as I listened to her—the heroic woman! A reward of $10,000 was offered for her by the Southerners, and her friends deemed it best that she sh'ld, for a time find refuge in Can.[ada]. And she did so, but only for a short time. She came back and was soon at the good brave work again....But she wants to go North, and will probably do so ere long. I am glad I saw her—*very* glad.

Source: Stevenson, p. 442.

Working as a scout and spy, Tubman gathered important information for the Union Army. She reported on enemy troop movements and the locations of their camps. In June of 1863, Tubman accompanied Colonel James Montgomery, who commanded the black regiment at Port Royal, on a gunboat raid along the Combahee River in

South Carolina. Troops in three gunboats were guided up river by Tubman and put ashore in rowboats. They raided and burned Confederate plantations and freed the slaves there. The Union troops met little resistance from rebel soldiers and the gunboats took the freed people on board and back behind Union lines. In all, more than 750 slaves were transported down river to freedom by the successful raid. Many of the men enlisted as soldiers under Montgomery. The rest established a settlement which they named Montgomery Hill. An article about the raid which appeared on the front page of the Boston Commonwealth newspaper on July 10, 1863 stated:

Col. Montgomery and his gallant band of black soldiers, under the guidance of a black woman, dashed into the enemy's country, struck a bold and effective blow...and brought off near 800 slaves....Many times she (Harriet) has penetrated the enemy's lines and discovered their situation and condition, and escaped without injury, but not without extreme hazard....

Sarah Emma Edmonds

Women as well as men risked their lives for the cause they believed in. The women profiled in this section put themselves in danger time and time again for the Union and for the Confederacy. One woman, in particular, not only went behind enemy lines as a spy but kept her female identity a secret while serving in the infantry as a man for more than two years.

Born in December 1841 in Salisbury, New Brunswick, Canada, Sarah Emma Edmonds grew up hunting, fishing, swimming, and shooting. Strong and tough, she tried hard to please her strict father, who preferred sons to daughters. It was her mother who taught Edmonds nursing skills.

At 17, Edmonds ran away from home to escape a marriage arranged by her father. Since women in the 19th century had limited rights, Edmonds cut her hair short and disguised herself as a man to keep her freedom and independence. As "Frank Thompson," Edmonds became a successful book salesman, first in St. John, New Brunswick and later in Hartford, Connecticut. In 1860, Edmonds, now known as a nice-looking and prosperous young man, moved to Flint, Michigan. It was there on April 17, 1861 that the 20-year-old enlisted in the 2nd regiment of Michigan volunteers as a male field nurse. The 2nd Michigan traveled immediately to Washington and became part of the Union's Army of the Potomac. It was not long before Edmonds was involved in the first great battle of the Civil War at Bull

Run on July 21, 1861. The following excerpts are from her autobiography, first published in 1864:

...The 17th of July dawned bright and clear, and everything being in readiness, the Army of the Potomac took up its line of march for Manassas [Bull Run]. In gay spirits the army moved forward, the air resounding with the music of the regimental bands, and patriotic songs of the soldiers. No gloomy forebodings seemed to damp the spirits of the men, for a moment, but "On to Richmond" was echoed and re-echoed, as that vast army moved rapidly over the country. I felt strangely out of harmony with the wild, joyous spirit which pervaded the troops. As I rode slowly along, watching those long lines of bayonets as they gleamed and flashed in the sunlight, I thought that many, very many, of those enthusiastic men who appeared so eager to meet the enemy, would never return to relate the success or defeat of that splendid army. Even if victory should perch upon their banners, and I had no doubt it would, yet many noble lives must be sacrificed ere it could be obtained....

...The first man I saw killed was a gunner belonging to Col. R.'s command. A shell had burst in the midst of the battery, killing one and wounding three men and two horses. Mr. B. [the chaplain] jumped from his horse, hitched it to a tree, and ran forward to the battery; Mrs. B. and I following his example as fast as we could. I stooped over one of the wounded, who lay upon his face weltering in his blood....He was mortally wounded in the breast, and the tide of life was fast ebbing away; the stretchers were soon brought, and he was carried from the field....

Now the battle began to rage with terrible fury. Nothing could be heard save the thunder of artillery, the clash of steel, and the continuous roar of musketry....There was no place of safety for miles around; the safest place was the post of duty. Many that day who turned their backs upon the enemy and sought refuge in the woods some two miles distant, were found torn to pieces by shell, or mangled by cannon ball—a proper reward for those who, insensible to shame, duty, or patriotism, desert their cause and comrades in the trying hour of battle and skulk away cringing under the fear of death.

Still the battle continues without cessation...the sight of that field is perfectly appalling; men tossing their arms wildly calling for help; there they lie bleeding, torn and mangled; legs, arms, and bodies are crushed and broken as if smitten by thunderbolts; the ground is crimson with blood; it is terrible to witness. Burnside's brigade is being mown down like grass by the rebel batteries; the men are not able to stand that terrible storm of shot and shell; they begin to waver and fall back slowly, but just at the right moment Capt. Sykes comes up to their relief with his command of regulars. They sweep up the hill where Burnside's exhausted, shattered brigade still lingers, and are greeted with a shout of joy, such as none but soldiers, who are almost overpowered by a fierce enemy, and are reinforced by their brave comrades, can give.

Onward they go, close up to the cloud of flame and smoke rolling from the hill upon which the rebel batteries are placed—their muskets are leveled—there is a click, click—a sheet of flame—a deep roll like that of thunder, and the rebel gunners are seen to stagger and fall. The guns become silent, and in a few moments are abandoned. This seems to occasion great confusion in the rebel ranks. Regiments were scattered, and officers were seen riding furiously and shouting their orders, which were heard above the roar and din of battle....

But just as our army is confident of success, and is following up the advantage which it has gained, rebel reinforcements arrive and turn the tide of battle. Two rebel regiments of fresh troops are sent to make a flank movement in order to capture Griffin's and Rickett's batteries. They march through the woods, reach the top of the hill, and form a line so completely in our rear as to fire almost upon the backs of the gunners.... Men and horses went down in an instant. A moment more and those famous batteries were in the hands of the enemy.

The news of this disaster spread along our lines like wildfire; officers and men were alike confounded; regiment after regiment broke and ran, and almost immediately the panic commenced....

Mrs. B. and I made our way to the stone church around which we saw stacks of dead bodies piled up, and arms and legs were thrown together in heaps. But how shall I describe the scene within the church at that hour? Oh, there was suffering there which no pen can ever describe. One case I can never forget. It was that of a poor fellow whose legs were both broken above the knees, and from the knees to the thighs they were literally smashed to fragments. He was dying; but oh, what a death was that. He was insane, perfectly wild, and required two persons to hold him. Inflammation had set in, and was rapidly doing its work; death soon released him, and it was a relief to all present as well as to the poor sufferer....

Our hearts and hands being fully occupied with such scenes as these, we thought of nothing else. We knew nothing of the true state of affairs outside, nor could we believe it possible when we learned that the whole army had retreated toward Washington, leaving the wounded in the hands of the enemy, and us, too, in rather an unpleasant situation....

Source: Sarah Emma Edmonds, *Memoirs of a Soldier, Nurse, and Spy* (DeKalb: Northern Illinois University Press, 1999), pp. 12, 16-21.

Belle Boyd

One of the most famous Confederate female spies during the Civil War was Belle Boyd. The daughter of a Shenandoah Valley storekeeper in Martinsburg, Virginia, Boyd was only 17 when she began to spy for the Confederacy. Arrested six times and imprisoned twice, Boyd's exploits were often reported in the newspapers. She is credited with helping her favorite general, Stonewall Jackson, lead a successful surprise atttack on Union forces at Front Royal, Virginia in May 1862.

The following excerpt from her wartime memoir, originally published in 1865, describes her experiences following her detention by Union forces on suspicion of espionage and subsequent release to return to her home in Virginia, which was occupied by Union troops:

...The night before the departure of [Union] General Shields, who was about, as he informed us, to "whip" Jackson, a council of war was held in what had formerly been my aunt's drawing-room. Immediately above this was a bed-chamber, containing a closet, through the floor of which I observed a hole had been bored, whether with a view to espionage or not I have never been able to ascertain. It occurred to me, however, that I might turn the discovery to account; and as soon as the council of war had

Belle Boyd.

assembled, I stole softly up stairs, and lying down on the floor of the closet, applied my ear to the hole, and found, to my great joy, I could distinctly hear the conversation that was passing below.

The council prolonged their discussion for some hours; but I remained motionless and silent until the proceedings were brought to a conclusion, at one o'clock in the morning. As soon as the coast was clear I crossed the court-yard, and made the best of my way to my own room, and took down in cipher everything I had heard which seemed to me of any importance.

I felt convinced that to rouse a servant, or make any disturbance at that hour, would excite the suspicions of the Federals by whom I was surrounded; accordingly I went straight to the stables myself, saddled my horse, and galloped away in the direction of the mountains.

Fortunately I had about me some passes which I had from time to time procured for Confederate soldiers returning south, and which, owing to various circumstances, had never been put in requisition. They now, however, proved invaluable; for I was twice brought to a standstill by the challenge of the Federal sentries, and who would inevitably have put a period to my adventurous career had they not been beguiled by my false passport. Once clear of the chain of sentries, I dashed on unquestioned across fields and along roads, through fens and marshes, until, after a scamper of about fifteen miles, I found myself at the door of Mr. M's house.

...I proceeded to narrate all I had overheard in the closet, of which I have before made mention. I gave [Confederate Colonel Ashby] the cipher, and started on my return.

I arrived safely at my aunt's house, after a two hours' ride, in the course of which I "ran the blockade" of a sleeping sentry, who awoke to the sound of my horse's hoofs just in time to see me disappear round an abrupt turning, which shielded me from the bullet he was about to send after me....

Source: Belle Boyd, *Belle Boyd in Camp and Prison* (South Brunswick: Thomas Yoseloff, 1968) pp. 150-52.

Later, Boyd discovered that Federal troops planned to destroy several important bridges after passing over them, as described in the following excerpt:

...I was in possession of much important information, which, if I could only contrive to convey to General Jackson, I knew our victory would be secure. Without it I had every reason to anticipate defeat and disaster.

I again went down to the door, and this time I observed, standing about in groups, several men who had always professed attachment to the cause of the South. I demanded if there was one among them who would venture to carry to General Jackson the information I possessed. They all with one accord said, "No, no. You go."

I did not stop to reflect. My heart, though beating fast, was not appalled. I put on a white sun-bonnet, and started at a run down the street, which was thronged with Federal officers and men. I soon cleared the town and gained the open fields, which I traversed with unabated speed, hoping to escape observation until such time as I could make good my way to the Confederate line, which was still rapidly advancing.

I had on a dark-blue dress, with a little fancy white apron over it; and the contrast of colors, being visible at a great distance, made me far more conspicuous than was just then agreeable....

My escape was most providential; for, although I was not hit, the rifle-balls flew thick and fast about me, and more than one struck the ground so near my feet as to throw the dust in my eyes. Nor was this all: the Federals [occupying] the hospital, seeing in what direction the shots of their pickets were aimed, followed the example and also opened fire upon me.

Upon this occasion my life was spared by what seemed to me then, and seems still, little short of a miracle; for, besides the numerous bullets that whistled by my ears, several actually pierced different parts of my clothing, but not one reached my body. Besides all this, I was exposed to a crossfire from the Federal and Confederate artillery, whose shot and shell flew whistling and hissing over my head.

At length a Federal shell struck the ground within twenty yards of my feet; and the explosion, of course, sent the fragments flying in every direction around me. I had, however, just time to throw myself flat upon the ground before the deadly engine burst; and again Providence spared my life.

Springing up when the danger was passed, I pursued my career, still under a heavy fire. I shall never run again as I ran on that, to me memorable day. Hope, fear, the love of life, and the determination to serve my country to the last, conspired to fill my heart with more than feminine courage, and to lend preternatural strength and swiftness to my limbs. I often marvel, and even shudder, when I reflect how I cleared the fields, and bounded over the fences with the agility of a deer....

...I caught sight of the main body fast approaching; and soon an old friend and connection of mine, Major Harry Douglas, rode up, and recognizing me, cried out, while he seized my hand—

"Good God, Belle, you here! What is it?"

...as soon as I had sufficiently recovered myself, I produced the "little note," and told him all, urging him to hurry on the cavalry, with orders to them to seize the bridges before the retreating Federals should have time to destroy them.

He instantly galloped off to report to General Jackson, who immediately rode forward, and asked me if I would have an escort and a horse wherewith to return to the village. I thanked him, and said, "No; I would go as I came;" and then, acting upon the information I had been spared to convey, the Confederates gained a most complete victory.

Though the depot building had been fired, and was burning, our cavalry reached the bridges barely in time to save them from destruction: the retreating Federals had just crossed, and were actually upon the point of lighting the slow match which, communicating with the bursting charge, would have riven the arches in pieces. So hasty was their retreat that they left all their killed and wounded in our hands.

Although we lost many of our best and bravest...the day was ours; and I had the heartfelt satisfaction to know that it was in consequence of the information I had conveyed at such risk to myself General Jackson made the flank movement which led to such fortunate results....

I could not but be aware that I had been of some service to my country; and I had the further satisfaction of feeling that neither a desire of fame nor notoriety had been my motive for enacting the role I did in this sad drama. I was not prepared, however, for that recognition of my services which was received on the very day they were rendered, and which I transcribe:—

"May 23d, 1862

Miss Belle Boyd,

I thank you, for myself and for the army, for the immense service that you have rendered your country to-day.

Hastily, I am your friend,
T.J. Jackson, C.S.A."

Source: Boyd, pp. 161-167.

Pauline Cushman

Born in New Orleans, Louisiana, Pauline Cushman was the daughter of a French mother and Spanish father. She left home at age 18 for a life in the theater and, by the time she was 20, was appearing on stages in cities throughout the country.

When the Civil War broke out in 1861, Cushman was a 28-year-old actress married to a fellow actor named Charles Dickinson. He enlisted in the Union Army as a musician but died after a short illness. Although a Southerner by birth, Cushman's sympathies were with the North.

In March of 1863, she was appearing in a production of "The Seven Sisters" at Wood's Theatre in Louisville, Kentucky. Although Kentucky was a Union state, the city of Louisville was filled with Southern supporters. Cushman was approached by two men who assumed the popular actress also supported the Confederate cause. They dared her to drink a toast to the South during her performance in one of the show's skits that night, and even offered her money.

Cushman visited Colonel Moore, the Federal Provost marshal in Louisville, for his opinion. Moore urged her to make the toast. Publicly, everyone would think Cushman was a Confederate but privately she could help identify spies and Southern sympathizers for the North.

That night's performance was standing room only. Cushman, following the performance of a skit, lifted a champagne glass in her hand and walked away from the other performers to the edge of the stage. Everyone was silent as she raised her glass to the audience and said loudly, "Here's to Jeff Davis and the Southern Confederacy. May the South always maintain her honor and her rights."

Shouts and cheers, mingled with boos and hisses, rang out in the theatre. Fights started in the audience. In one night, Pauline Cushman had become a Southern heroine. No one suspected her of being a Federal spy and, in the months that followed, her fame spread. People flocked to theaters in Louisville and Nashville to see her perform. Southerners rushed to her side, confiding Confederate secrets and important information. For months, she passed on this valuable material to Union officials.

One day, Colonel William Truesdail, head of intelligence for the Union's Army of the Cumberland, gave Cushman her most dangerous assignment. She was to visit the camps of Confederate General Bragg and the Army of Tennessee and obtain all the information she could about troop numbers, movements, and fortifications. Her excuse in visiting was that she was searching for her long lost brother (who really was a member of the Confederate army). Truesdail's order to Cushman was to remember everything and put nothing down on paper.

It was May of 1863 when the young actress was escorted out of the city of Nashville with other women who were suspected of aiding the Confederate cause. Her fame gave Cushman immediate access behind Confederate lines. She befriended Rebel officers, who talked to her openly about military strategy, troop movements, and regiment strength.

Living a spy's life finally caught up with Cushman. Disobeying orders, she made notes and drawings and stole enemy blueprints, which she hid in the lining of her shoes. Cushman was caught once and escaped, then caught again. The papers were found and used as evidence against her.

Cushman was tried before General Bragg and a military court, found guilty, and sentenced to death by hanging. A few days later, Union forces attacked Bragg and the Rebels pulled out quickly, retreating south to Chattanooga. In the confusion, Cushman was left behind. Upon her liberation by Union soldiers, she gave the Union officers valuable information about what she had seen and heard before her capture.

Rebel Rose

A native of Maryland who grew up in Washington, Rose O'Neal Greenhow was a strong secessionist and devoted to the Southern cause. When her husband, Dr. Robert Greenhow, died in 1854, Rose Greenhow used her political friendships and influence to support herself and her four daughters. She knew senators, generals, congressmen, and statesmen from both the North and the South. Even President James Buchanan was a frequent visitor to her home.

The widow was always surrounded by male admirers, and when the Civil War broke out, Rose Greenhow used her position as a famous Washington hostess to obtain important information for the South. Within weeks, she was the head of a secret spy ring and was directly

Rose O'Neal Greenhow and her daughter.

responsible for General Beauregard's Confederate victory at the battle of Bull Run (First Manassas) in July of 1861. The "Rebel Rose," as she was called, supplied important dates and information to Beauregard in several messages.

Shortly after the Confederate victory, Greenhow was placed under house arrest by the Federal government for five months. In January 1862 she was transferred to Old Capitol Prison, where she remained until her release on June 2, 1862. At that time, she signed a document promising "not to return north of the Potomac River during the present hostilities without the permission of the Secretary of War of the United States."

When Greenhow arrived in the Confederate capitol of Richmond, Virginia on June 4, Confederate President Jefferson Davis declared, "But for you there would have been no battle of Bull Run." The successful spy was next sent as an ambassador to England and France in order to gather support for the Confederate cause. While returning from that mission to Europe in 1864, Greenhow drowned when the boat which was rowing her ashore overturned.

Greenhow wrote of her experiences in her book, My Imprisonment and the First Year of Abolition Rule, *excerpts from which follow:*

On the morning of the 16th of July, 1861, the Government papers at Washington announced that the [Union] "grand army" was in motion and I learned from a reliable source (having received a copy of the order to McDowell) that the order for a forward movement had gone forth....

At twelve o'clock on the morning of the 16th
of July, I dispatched a messenger to Manassas,
who arrived there at eight o'clock that night. The
answer received by me at mid-day on the 17th will
tell the purport of my communication—

"Yours was received at eight oclock [sic] at night.
Let them come: we are ready for them. We rely upon
you for   precise information. Be particular as to
description and destination of forces, quantity of
artillery etc."

Signed, "Thomas Jordan, Adjt Gen."

On the 17th of July, I dispatched another
message to Manassas, for I had learned of the
intention of the enemy to cut the Winchester railroad,
so as to intercept Johnston and prevent his reinforcing
Beauregard who had comparatively but a small
force under his command at Manassas....

On Sunday (21st) the great battle of Manassas
was fought—which ended in the total defeat of
the entire "Grand Army." In the world's history
such a sight was never witnessed: statesmen, Senators,
Congressmen, generals and officers of every grade,
soldiers, teamsters—all rushing in frantic fright,
as if pursued by countless demons....The news of
the disastrous rout of the Yankee Army was cried

through the streets of New York on the 22nd. The whole city seemed paralyzed by fear....

...On Friday, Aug. 23, 1861, as I was entering my own door in returning from a promenade, I was arrested by two men, one in citizens clothes and the other in the dress of an officer of the United States Army. This latter was called Major Allen, and was the chief of the detective police of the city. They followed close upon my footsteps. As I ascended my steps the two men ascended also before I could open the door and asked, "Is this Mrs. Greenhow?" I answered "Yes." "Who are you and what do you want?" "I come to arrest you"—"By what authority?" The man Allen, or Pinkerton (for he had several aliases) said: "By sufficient authority." I said: "Let me see your warrant." He mumbled something about verbal authority from the War and State Department and then they followed me into the house. By this time the house had become filled with men, and men also surrounded it outside like bees from a hive. An indiscriminate search now commenced throughout my house. Men rushed with frantic haste into my chamber. My beds, my wardrobes were all upturned. My library was taken possession of and every scrap of paper was seized....

The work of examining my papers had commenced. I had no reason to fear of the consequences from the papers which had as yet fallen into their hands. I had a right to my own political opinions. I am a Southern woman, born with Revolutionary blood in my veins, Freedom of speech and of thought were my birthright, guaranteed, signed and sealed by the blood of our fathers.

...I was allowed to go to my chamber and I then resolved to destroy some important papers which I had in my pocket, even at the expense of my life. (The papers were my cipher, with which I corresponded with my friends at Manassas.) Happily I succeeded without such a painful sacrifice....

A very large sum had been offered for my cipher. This stimulated the zeal of the employees of the Government to a very remarkable degree. The tables were filled with fragments of old letters and scraps in cipher, in several languages, from early morning till late at night. For seven days they puzzled over them. I had no fear. —One by one they allowed the clue to escape them. Only once was I frightened. Miss Mackall, who like myself was always on the alert, abstracted from a heap of papers a sheet of blotting paper upon which was the whole of my dispatch to Manassas on July 16.

On Friday the 30th of August I was informed that my house was to be converted into a prison....

Source: Rose O'Neal Greenhow, *My Imprisonment and the First Year of Abolition Rule at Washington* (1864), *reprinted in* Katharine M. Jones, *Heroines of Dixie* (Indianapolis: Bobbs-Merrill Company, 1955), pp. 62-66.

Elizabeth Van Lew:
Federal Spy in Richmond

The daughter of a wealthy hardware merchant and slaveholder, Elizabeth Van Lew grew up in Richmond, Virginia. She was educated in Philadelphia and returned home opposed to slavery. "Slave power crushes freedom of speech and of opinion," she wrote in her diary. "Slave power degrades labor. Slave power is arrogant, is jealous...is despotic, not only over the slave but over the community, [and] the state." When her father died in 1860, Van Lew and her mother freed the nine family slaves, many of whom chose to remain at their jobs.

As an open abolitionist in Richmond, Van Lew was an outsider in the community and looked upon as strange and suspicious by her neighbors. When the war began, she became an active spy for the Union.

Van Lew and her mother made daily visits to Federal captives at Libby Prison, carrying food baskets, medicine, and books. She gathered military information from Union prisoners about Confederate troop movements and artillery strength. She even used her house servants as couriers and sent them north with coded messages in their boots or in their clothing.

Since the Van Lews were well-known and wealthy citizens, a Richmond newspaper wrote an article about "their shocking activities" and "attentions to the Yankee prisoners," as follows:

Two ladies, mother and daughter, living on Church Hill, have lately attracted public notice by their....attentions to the Yankee prisoners...Whilst every true woman in this community has been busy making articles for our troops, or administering to our sick, these two women have been spending their opulent means in aiding and giving comfort to the miscreants who have invaded our sacred soil...The course of these two females, in providing them with delicacies, bringing them books, stationery and paper, cannot but be regarded as an evidence of sympathy amounting to an endorsement of the cause and conduct of these Northern vandals.

One of the Van Lews' ex-slaves, Mary Elizabeth Bowser, had been sent North to be educated before the war at the Van Lews' expense. She now lived outside of Richmond and Elizabeth Van Lew turned to her for help. The young woman was able to get a job within the household staff of Jefferson Davis. Thanks to Van Lew, the Union now had a spy in the home of the Confederate President.

With the help of other Union supporters in the Richmond area, Van Lew set up a courier system with five relay stations to send messages to the North. Throughout the war, Van Lew provided accurate military information to Union Generals Butler and Grant. She also aided captured Union soldiers who escaped from Confederate prisons and used secret rooms, staircases, and tunnels to hide them in her mansion.

According to General George Sharpe of the Army Intelligence Bureau, Elizabeth Van Lew "represented all that was left of the power of the United States government in the city of Richmond."

When Grant was finally preparing to enter the city in 1865, Van Lew rushed to the roof of her mansion and unfurled the Stars and Stripes. Angry Southerners surrounded her house and threatened to destroy it. The petite 47-year-old spy faced them down and shouted, "I know you, and you, and you," pointing to her neighbors and other community members. "General Grant will be in this city within the hour; if this house is harmed, your houses shall be burned by noon." The crowd walked away and the Van Lews were left alone.

One of the first things General Grant did after taking Richmond was to visit Elizabeth Van Lew and provide protection for the family. Later, when Grant became President (1869-1877), he appointed her postmistress of Richmond, where she lived until her death in 1900. Van Lew's neighbors never forgave her support for the Union. Most still avoided and ignored her years after the Civil War.

An excerpt from the diary of Elizabeth Van Lew demonstrates her social isolation, as follows:

...The threats, the scowls, the frowns of an infuriated community—who can write them? I have had brave men shake their fingers in my face and say terrible things. We had threats of being driven away, threats of fire, and threats of death. "You dare to show sympathy for any of these prisoners," said a gentleman, shaking his finger in my face. "I would shoot them as I would blackbirds—and there is something on foot against you *now!*"..." One day I could speak for my country, the next I was threatened with death. Surely madness was upon the people!...

Source: Katharine M. Jones, *Ladies of Richmond* (Indianapolis: Bobbs-Merrill Company, 1962), p. 198.

The following is the text from a cipher letter from Van Lew to General Benjamin F. Butler, setting forth information about the Confederate forces in Richmond:

January 30, 1864

To (Union) General Benjamin F. Butler:

Dear Sir: It is intended to remove to Georgia very soon all the Federal prisoners; butchers and bakers to go at once. They are already notified and selected. Quaker [a Union man whom I know...] knows this to be true. Are building batteries on the Danville road.

This from Quaker: Beware of new and rash council! Beware! This I send you by direction of all your friends. No attempt should be made with less than 30,000 cavalry, from 10,000 to 15,000 infantry to support them, amounting in all to 40,000 to 45,000 troops. Do not underrate their strength and desperation. Forces could probably be called into action in from 5 to 10 days; 25,000 mostly artillery Hoke's and Kemper's brigades gone to North Carolina; Pickett's in or about Petersburg. Three regiments of cavalry disbanded by General Lee for want of horses. Morgan is applying for 1,000 choice men for a raid.

Source: Jones, *Ladies of Richmond*, pp. 199-200.

Another excerpt from Van Lew's diary, describing the arrival of Union troops in Richmond, follows:

Sunday April 2, 1865....Night came on. We could hear the hurried leaving. Word was sent us that our house was to be burned—some Confederate soldiers had said so....

The constant explosion of shells, the blowing up of the gunboats, and of the powder magazine, seemed to jar, to shake the earth, and lend a mighty language to the scene. All nature trembled at the work of arbitrary powers, the consummation of the wrongs of years; the burning bridges, the roaring flames added a wild grandeur to the scene.

Amid all this turmoil, quietly, noiselessly, the Federal army entered the city. There were wild bursts of welcome from the Negroes and many whites as they poured in. In an incredibly short space of time by magic every part of our city was under the most kind and respectful of guards. What a moment!

No wonder the walls of our house were swaying; the heart of our city a flaming altar, as His mighty work was done. Oh! army of my country, how glorious was your welcome!

Source: Jones, *Ladies of Richmond,* pp. 279-280.

Louisa May Alcott

Nursing the wounded and administering aid and supplies contributed greatly to military success and troop morale during the Civil War. Thousands of women served as volunteer nurses in both the North and South. They were faced with overwhelming casualties, crowded and unclean conditions, and widespread disease. For most,

Louisa May Alcott.

it was an unforgettable experience. Author Louisa May Alcott worked at the Union Hospital in the Georgetown area of Washington in January and February of 1863. She was at the hospital for six weeks when a "severe attack of fever" forced her to return to her home in Concord, Massachusetts. Alcott's letters to her family, detailing her experiences as a volunteer nurse, were first printed in the "Commonwealth" newspaper and later in a book entitled Hospital Sketches. *Excerpts from* Hospital Sketches *follow:*

> The first thing I met was a regiment of the vilest odors that ever assaulted the human nose...and the worst of this affliction was, everyone had assured me

that it was a chronic weakness of all hospitals, and I must bear it. I did, armed with lavender water, with which I so besprinkled myself and premises, that I was soon known among my patients as "the nurse with the bottle."...I progressed by slow stages up stairs and down, till the main hall was reached, and I paused to take breath and a survey. There they were! "our brave boys," as the papers justly call them, for cowards could hardly have been so riddled with shot and shell, so torn and shattered, nor have borne suffering for which we have no name, with an uncomplaining fortitude, which made one glad to cherish each as a brother. In they came, some on stretchers, some in men's arms, some feebly staggering along propped on rude crutches, and one lay stark and still with covered face, as a comrade gave his name to be recorded before they carried him away to the dead house. All was hurry and confusion; the hall was full of these wrecks of humanity, for the most exhausted could not reach a bed till duly ticketed and registered; the walls were lined with rows of such as could sit, the floor covered with the more disabled, the steps and doorways filled with helpers and lookers on; the sound of many feet and voices made that usually quiet hour as noisy as noon; and, in the midst of it all, the matron's motherly face brought more comfort to many a poor soul, than the cordial draughts she administered, or the cheery words that welcomed all, making of the hospital a home.

The sight of several stretchers, each with its legless, armless, or desperately wounded occupant, entering my ward, admonished me that I was there to work, not to wonder or weep; so I corked up my feelings, and returned to the path of duty, which was rather "a hard road to travel" just then. The house had been a hotel before hospitals were needed, and many of the doors still bore their old names; some not so inappropriate as might be imagined, for my ward was in truth a *ball-room*, if gun-shot wounds could christen it. Forty beds were prepared, many already tenanted by tired men who fell down anywhere, and drowsed till the smell of food roused them. Round the great stove was gathered the dreariest group I ever saw—ragged, gaunt and pale, mud to the knees, with bloody bandages untouched since put on days before; many bundled up in blankets, coats being lost or useless; and all wearing that disheartened look which proclaimed defeat....I pitied them so much, I dared not speak to them, though, remembering all they had been through since the fight at Fredericksburg, I yearned to serve the dreariest of them all. Presently, Miss Blank tore me from my refuge behind piles of one-sleeved shirts, odd socks, bandages and lint; put basin, sponge, towels and a block of brown soap into my hands, with these appalling directions:

"Come, my dear, begin to wash as fast you can. Tell them to take off socks, coats, and shirts, scrub them well, put on clean shirts, and the attendants will finish them off, and lay them in bed."

If she had requested me to shave them all, or dance a hornpipe on the stove funnel, I should have been less staggered; but to scrub some dozen lords of creation at a moment's notice, was really—really—. However, there was no time for nonsense, and, having resolved when I came to do everything I was bid, I drowned my scruples in my wash-bowl, clutched my soap manfully, and, assuming a business-like air, made a dab at the first dirty specimen I saw...

Source: Louisa May Alcott, *Hospital Sketches* (Bedford, MA: Applewood Books, 1993), pp. 27-29.

Kate Cumming

*Twenty-eight year old Kate Cumming lived in
Mobile, Alabama when the Civil War began. She served
as a volunteer nurse in the hospital division of the Army
of Tennessee until fighting ended in 1865. The following
are excerpts from the journal in which she chronicled
her experiences:*

April 11, 1862.—...Mrs. Ogden tried to prepare
me for the scenes which I should witness upon
entering the wards. But alas! nothing that I had ever
heard or read had given me the faintest idea of the
horrors witnessed here. I do not think that words
are in our vocabulary expressive enough to present
to the mind the realities of that sad scene. Certainly,
none of the glories of the war were presented here.
But I must not say that; for if uncomplaining
endurance is glory, we had plenty of it. If that is
what makes the hero, here they were by scores.
Gray-haired men—men in the pride of manhood—
beardless boys—Federals and all, mutilated in every
imaginable way, lying on the floor, just as they were
taken from the battle-field; so close together that it
was almost impossible to walk without stepping on
them. I could not command my feelings enough to
speak, but thoughts crowded upon me. O, if the

authors of this cruel and unnatural war could but see what I saw there, they would try and put a stop to it! To think, that it is man who is working all this woe upon his fellow man. What can be in the minds of our enemies, who are now arrayed against us, who have never harmed them in any way, but simply claim our own, and nothing more! May God forgive them, for surely they know not what they do.

...If I were to live a hundred years, I should never forget the poor sufferers' gratitude; for every little thing, done for them—a little water to drink, or the bathing of their wounds—seemed to afford them the greatest relief.

The Federal prisoners are receiving the same attention as our men. They are lying side by side. Many are just being brought in from the battle-field....

April 12.—I sat up all night, bathing the men's wounds, and giving them water. Every one attending to them seemed completely worn out. Some of the doctors told me that they had scarcely slept since the battle. As far as I have seen, the surgeons are very kind to the wounded, and nurse as well as doctor them.

The men are lying all over the house, on their blankets, just as they were brought from the battle-field. They are in the hall, on the gallery, and crowded into very small rooms. The foul air from this mass of human beings at first made me giddy and sick, but I soon got over it. We have to walk, and when we give the men any thing kneel, in blood and water; but we think nothing of it at all. There was much suffering among the patients last night; one old man groaned all the time....

April 23.—A young man whom I have been attending is going to have his arm cut off. Poor fellow! I am doing all that I can to cheer him. He says that he knows that he will die, as all who have had limbs amputated in this hospital have died. It is but too true; such is the case. It is said that the reason is that none but the very worst cases are left here, and they are too far gone to survive the shock which the operation gives the frame....

April 24.— Mr. Isaac Fuquet, the young man who had his arm cut off, died to-day. He lived only a few hours after the amputation. The operation was performed by Surgeon Chaupin of New Orleans, whose professional abilities are very highly commended. Dr. Hereford was well acquainted with Mr. Fuquet and intends to inform his mother of his death....

May 23.—...One of the saddest sights witnessed are two Federals, who have been here since the battle of Shiloh. One has had his arm, the other his leg amputated. They are seventeen and eighteen years of age, respectively. They look very pitiful, dying among strangers, far away from their own homes and relatives. They have been cared for the same as our own; but that is not all that is wanted. They need sympathy, and of that character which it is impossible for us to extend to them, as they came here with the full intention of taking all that is dear to us. They may have been conscientious, and thought that they were doing their duty, but we are of a different opinion, and it will be some time before we change. They will soon die; both are religious. I never look at them without thinking of the thousands of our poor men who are in the same condition in the North. I do sincerely trust that they are as well treated as these poor fellows have been.

Source: Kate Cumming, *Kate: The Journal of a Confederate Nurse* (Baton Rouge: Louisiana State University Press, 1959), pp. 14-15, 24-25, 39.

Hannah Ropes

A homemaker and political activist, New Englander Hannah Ropes was a strong abolitionist and supporter of the Union when the Civil War broke out. Along with Louisa May Alcott, she worked as a volunteer nurse at the Union Hotel Hospital in Washington from June 1862 until her untimely death in January 1863. In the short period she was a military nurse, Hannah worked nonstop to improve overall conditions at the hospital. Her efforts resulted in a change of administration, better sanitary conditions and cleanliness, increased food and supplies, and regular inspections. The following are excerpts from Ropes' diary and letters:

October 6, 1862

Dear Alice—

...The men have not had enough to eat for a week—this morning, one slice of bread to each man! As soon as I found it out, I took a half bushel of apples and...told the men if I could have my way they should have more than enough, and I hoped the steward would go hungry sometime. They gathered round me as thick as chickens and [ate] their apples. It was all I had from a barrel sent me. Tell the country people to dry all the apples they can for the soldiers.

I have stopped again, Alice, to close the eyes of a gentle German boy who has no one in this country to mourn for him. His parents live in the father land, and all the record there will be is a number on his grave...

Your Mother

November 6, 1862. The day drags heavily. I was up in the night to go my rounds; the half lit halls, the cold floors, and over all the sense of universal depression in the house made me feel as though I was all alone. I mounted to the third floor to look after some sick patients. One who I left, feeling as though he might not live through the night, I turned my steps to. He seemed as I left him. I took a chair by him, for the weary watcher had fallen asleep on the floor. Why should he not? He is but a convalescent patient, and instead of watching, why should he not be resting? This lad is the only son of his mother and she a widow;

he is unable to speak, and has been so from the time he came into the house. I go from him to others, and as the clock strikes four I go back to bed. Miss Low is in the same room with me. I am glad though she is asleep, for it takes away the edge of my loneliness. When the day dawns one of my men has gone, and before the hour of supper time comes we close the eyes of two more, one the only son of his mother!...

Miss Kendall is driven nearly frantic over the small amount of food for her ward. Today she said she did not know but she might have one more week of three meals each day, to be created out of *"nothing,"* but a longer time was not to be thought of.

The matter of food is bad enough, but I believe the depressing sphere of the house tells quite as much upon the men as anything else. Generally I have been able to bring a smile from the invalids, but now they curl their heads under the sheet and think it is of no use to try any longer to get well....

Source: John R. Brumgardt, ed., *Civil War Nurse: The Diary and Letters of Hannah Ropes* (Knoxville: The University of Tennessee Press, 1980), pp. 69-70, 89-91.

Sophronia Bucklin

Women of all ages from various walks of life volunteered during the war as military nurses. Many kept diaries and journals of their experiences, and a number of them were published in book form years later. Sophronia Bucklin, a young schoolteacher from New York, and Fannie Beers, a married woman whose husband served in the Confederate Army, were both eyewitnesses to the horror and sufferings of battle. The writings of these two women reflect the awful realities of war in which more men died from disease and infection than from their wounds in battle.

In her book, In Hospital and Camp *(1869), Bucklin described her experience as a nurse at Judiciary Square Hospital, excerpts from which follow:*

> Our duties here were to distribute food to the patients, when brought up from the kitchen; wash the faces and hands, and comb the heads of the wounded; see that their bedding and clothing was kept clean and whole, bring pocket handkerchiefs, prepare and give the various drinks and stimulants at such times as they were ordered by the surgeon.
>
> I dropped into my desired sphere at once, and my whole soul was in the work. Every man wore the look of a hero in my eyes, for had they not

faced the red death from thundering artillery, and braved the deadly shots of the "minnies?" Had they not stood fearlessly, when like leaves of the autumn before a howling blast, they had fallen thick and fast—bronzed and dripping with gore—faces forward in the black mud of the trenches?

Source: Sophronia E. Bucklin, *In Hospital and Camp* (Philadelphia: John E. Potter and Company, 1869), reprinted in Harold E. Straubing, *In Hospital and Camp* (Harrisburg: Stackpole Books, 1993), pp. 102-03.

A few tents were up, for shelter, and, as fast as they were vacated by transportation to Washington, they were filled up from the numbers who were lying upon the ground, waiting to have their wounds dressed. A general and hurried care was exercised for their many and pressing wants—it was all we could under the circumstances afford them.

Death met us on every hand....Scenes of fresh horror rose up before us each day. Tales of suffering were told, which elsewhere would have well-nigh frozen the blood with horror. We grew callous to the sight of blood....

Often [the soldiers] would long for a drink of clear, cold water, and lie on the hard ground, straining the filthy river water through closely set teeth.

So tortured were we all, in fact, by this thirst...
that even now, when I lift to my lips a drink of
pure, cold water, I cannot swallow it without
thanking God for the priceless gift....

...Tents were being spread, and the ambulances
came upon the field with their ghastly, bloody
freight—unloading them, dying and groaning
under the sun—the small number of tents being
entirely insufficient to shelter the constantly
arriving throngs....

Men lay all around me, who had been left
for days on the battleground, wet with the dews of
night, disfigured with powder and dirt, with blood
oozing from their torn flesh, and worms literally
covering the festering wounds—dying with thirst,
starving for food, unable to attend to nature's
wants, groaning in delirious fever, praying to die,
to be rid of the intense pain which wracked the
poor body.

Such dreadful suffering I hope never to witness
again. The field was one vast plain of intense mortal
agony, tortured by the sun, and chilled by the night
dews. Everywhere were groans and cries for help;
everywhere were the pleading and glassy eyes of
dying men who were speechless in the delirium of

death. It was a scene to appall the stoutest hearts, but the excitement nerved us to shut our senses to everything but the task of relieving them as fast as possible. The dead lay by the living; the dying groaned by the dead, and still one hundred ambulances poured the awful tide in upon us....

Source: Sylvia Dannett, ed., *Noble Women of the North* (New York: Thomas Yoseloff Publishers, 1959), pp. 99-101, 171-173.

Fannie Beers

In her account, Memories. A Record of Personal Experience and Adventure During Four Years of War, *Fannie Beers wrote of her experiences as a Confederate army nurse in Newnan, Georgia:*

I was busy in one of the wards, when a messenger drove up, and a note was handed me from Dr. McAllister,—

"Some of our men too badly wounded to be moved right away. Come out at once. Bring cordials and brandy,—soup, if you have it,—also fill the enclosed requisition at the drug-store. Lose no time."

The battle-field was not three miles away. I was soon tearing along the road at breakneck speed. At an improvised field-hospital I met the doctor, who vainly tried to prepare me for the horrid spectacle I was about to witness.

From the hospital-tent distressing groans and screams came forth. The surgeons, both Confederate and Federal, were busy, with coats off, sleeves rolled up, shirtfronts and hands bloody. But our work lay not here.

Dr. McAllister silently handed me two canteens of water, which I threw over my shoulder, receiving also a bottle of peach brandy. We then turned into a ploughed field, thickly strewn with men and horses, many stone dead, some struggling in the agonies of death....

The dead lay around us on every side, singly and in groups and *piles;* men and horses, in some cases, apparently inextricably mingled. Some lay as if peacefully sleeping; others, with open eyes, seemed to glare at any who bent above them. Two men lay as they had died, the "Blue" and the "Gray," clasped in a fierce embrace. What had passed between them could never be known; but one was shot in the head, the throat of the other was partly torn away. It was awful to feel the conviction that unquenched hatred had embittered the last moments of each. They seemed mere youths, and I thought sadly of the mothers, whose hearts would throb with equal anguish in a Northern and a Southern home. In a corner of the field, supported by a pile of broken fence-rails, a soldier sat apparently beckoning to us. On approaching him we discovered that he was quite dead, although he sat upright, with open eyes and extended arm.

Several badly wounded men had been laid under the shade of some bushes a little farther on; our mission lay here. The portion of the field we crossed to reach this spot was in many places slippery with blood. The edge of my dress was red, my feet were wet with it. As we drew near the suffering men, piteous glances met our own. "Water! water!" was the cry....

...My hands and dress and feet were bloody, and I felt sick with horror.

Source: Fannie A. Beers, *Memories. A Record of Personal Experience and Adventure During Four Years of War* (Philadelphia: J.B. Lippincott Company, 1888), pp. 152-154.

Mother Bickerdyke

Mary Ann Bickerdyke of Illinois had the rare combination of being an excellent nurse as well as an organized and ambitious administrator. She was a forty-four year old widow and mother of three children when the Civil War began. Assigned to military hospitals in Cairo, Illinois, and the Gayoso Hospital in Memphis, Tennessee, among others, Bickerdyke nursed thousands of Union soldiers on the battlefield, in camp, and in hospitals everywhere. They were "her boys" and she was "Mother Bickerdyke" to them all.

Faced with unclean conditions and a lack of food and supplies, Mother Bickerdyke went to work immediately. She scrubbed and washed and cooked and went over the heads of the doctors in charge to demand clean bedding, proper medication, hospital clothing, and special diets for the sick and the wounded.

Bickerdyke confronted doctors directly and one senior surgeon went so far as to order her out of the hospital. According to the account of union army nurse and author Mary Livermore, Bickerdyke replied that "she should stay as long as the men needed her—that if he put her out of one door she should come in at another; and if he barred all the doors against her, she should come in at the windows, and that the patients would help her in. When anybody left it would be he, and not she...as she had already lodged complaints against him at headquarters." (Mary

A. *Livermore,* My Story of the War *(Hartford: A.D. Worthington and Company, 1888), p. 480.)*

Livermore described another encounter between Bickerdyke and an Army doctor, as follows:

One of the surgeons went to the rear with a wounded man, and found [Bickerdyke] wrapped in the gray overcoat of a rebel officer, for she had disposed of her blanket shawl to some poor fellow who needed it. She was wearing a soft slouch hat, having lost her inevitable Shaker bonnet. Her kettles had been set up, the fire kindled underneath, and she was dispensing hot soup, tea, crackers, panado, whiskey and water, and other refreshments, to the shivering, fainting, wounded men.

"Where did you get these articles?" [the surgeon] inquired; "and under whose authority are you at work?"

She paid no heed to his interrogatories, and, indeed, did not hear them, so completely absorbed was she in her work of compassion. Watching her with admiration for her skill, administrative ability, and intelligence,—for she not only fed the wounded men, but temporarily dressed their wounds in some cases,—he approached her again:—

"Madam, you seem to combine in yourself a sick-diet kitchen and a medical staff. May I inquire under whose authority you are working?"

Without pausing in her work, she answered him, "I have received my authority from the Lord God Almighty. Have you anything that ranks higher than that?" The truth was, she held no position whatever at that time. She was only a "volunteer nurse," having received no appointment, and being attached to no corps of relief.

Source: Livermore, pp. 489-90.

Mother Bickerdyke's reputation grew and she counted among her friends and supporters top Union generals such as Grant, Sherman, Logan, and Hurlbut. According to author Nina Brown Baker, a complaint lodged by a colonel against Bickerdyke was met by General Sherman with the response, "You've picked the one person around here who outranks me. If you want to lodge a complaint against her, you'll have to take it to President Lincoln." (Nina Brown Baker, Cyclone in Calico *(Boston: Little, Brown and Company, 1952), p. 160.)*

While in charge of the Gayoso Hospital in Tennessee, Mother Bickerdyke made several trips to Chicago and other major cities to collect money and aid for the sick and wounded. In Milwaukee, Wisconsin, the Chamber of Commerce pledged $1,200 a month for hospital relief and thanked Bickerdyke for her efforts in caring for Wisconsin boys in the war. Her reply, chronicled by

"I am much obliged to you, gentlemen," she answered, "for the kind things you have said. I haven't done much, no more than I ought; neither have you. I am glad you are going to give twelve hundred dollars a month for the poor fellows in the hospitals; for it's no more than you ought to do, and it isn't half as much as the soldiers in the hospitals have given for you. Suppose, gentlemen, you had got to give to-night one thousand dollars or your right leg, would it take long to decide which to surrender? Two thousand dollars or your right arm; five thousand dollars or both your eyes; all that you are worth or your life?

"But I have got eighteen hundred boys in my hospital at Chattanooga who have given one arm, and one leg, and some have given both, and yet they don't seem to think they have done a great deal for their country. And the graveyard behind the hospital, and the battle-field a little farther off, contain the bodies of thousands who have freely given their lives to save you and your homes and your country from ruin. Oh, gentlemen of Milwaukee, don't let us be telling of what we have given, and what we have done! We have done nothing, and given nothing, in comparison with *them*! And it's our duty to keep on giving and doing just as long as there's a soldier down South fighting or suffering for us."

Source: Livermore, pp. 531-32.

Mary Todd Lincoln

Keeping the home fires burning was often as important as the fighting on the battlefield. From the first ladies of the land, to the average 19th century woman experiencing the ravages of wartime, to female slaves on the plantation, the perspective of what it was like "back home" for these women differed markedly from one another. Mary Todd Lincoln, First Lady of the United States, and Varina Howell Davis, First Lady of the Confederacy, shared many similarities yet never met each other. Both were well-educated and intelligent women. Both shared the burdens and responsibilities of their husbands' high office, and both were loyal supporters of their respective causes. Both women suffered personal tragedy during the Civil War years with the loss of a child. Although Mary Lincoln experienced the triumph of a Union victory, her beloved husband, the source of her strength and courage, was murdered only five days later. Mary's life and fragile emotional state was never the same after Lincoln's assassination.

Varina Davis experienced the defeat of the South and the imprisonment of her husband, Jefferson Davis. Her efforts to free him in the years after the war were eventually successful and she went on to write a two-volume book of his life.

When the war began, Mary Lincoln routinely reviewed the troops and visited Washington hospitals. The Washington newspapers wrote, "Among the many ladies who visit the hospitals, none is more indefatigable than Mrs. Lincoln." The First Lady chatted with wounded soldiers, read books and wrote letters for them, and organized holiday meals. The only known letter written by Mrs. Lincoln for a soldier is as follows:

Campbell Hospital
Washington, D.C.
Aug 10th 1864

My dear Mrs. Agen—

I am sitting by the side of your soldier boy. He has been quite sick, but is getting well. He tells me to say to you that he is all right. With respect for the mother of the young soldier.

Mrs. Abraham Lincoln

Source: Justin G. Turner and Linda Levitt Turner, *Mary Todd Lincoln: Her Life and Letters* (New York: Alfred A. Knopf, Inc., 1972), p. 179.

At the same time, Mary Lincoln hosted lavish dinner parties in Washington and made numerous shopping trips to Philadelphia and New York to buy clothes, rugs, curtains, glassware and other items to redecorate the White House. Mary Lincoln was criticized in the press for

her extravagant spending habits. By 1865, she was nearly
$10,000 in debt.

Ex-slave and seamstress Elizabeth Keckley worked for
Mary Lincoln at the White House and became her closest
friend. In 1863, the First Lady joined with Keckley in
raising money for the Contraband Relief Society.
(Contraband was the name used for freed slaves.) Since
the start of the war, thousands of freed people had fled
from Virginia to Washington, settling in a small district of
the city which swelled in population from 1,800 ex-slaves
to 15,000 by 1863. Poverty was widespread in this area.
In a November 3, 1862 letter to her husband, who was
then away from Washington, D.C., Mrs. Lincoln wrote
as follows:

My dear Husband—

   I wrote you on yesterday, yet omitted a very
important item. Elizabeth Keckley, who is with me
and is working for the Contraband Association at
Wash[ington] is authorized by the *White* part of the
concern by a written document—to collect any thing
for them—*here* that, she can—She has been very
unsuccessful—She says the immense number of
Contrabands in W[ashington] are suffering intensely,
many without bed covering & having to use any bits
of carpeting to cover themselves—Many dying of
want—Out of the $1000 fund deposited with you by

General [Michael?] Corcoran, I have given her the privilege of investing $200 her[e] in bed covering. She is the most deeply grateful being, I ever saw, & this sum, I am sure, you will not object to being used in this way—The cause of humanity requires it—...

Source: Turner and Levitt Turner, pp. 140-41.

Varina Howell Davis

In a May 22, 1864 letter to her mother, Margaret Louisa Kempe Howell, Varina Davis wrote as follows:

...Jeff as you surmise has been forced from home constantly, and in the various battles around Richmond has been pretty constantly upon the field....Jeff is much worried by anxiety. He seems to have gotten nearly as bad as I am and I hear the roar of artillery and crack of muskets it seems to me all the time.

There is an immense deal of suffering here now, so much so that they are impressing servants in the street to nurse the wounded....and there are many deaths from slight wounds....

Source: Jones, *Ladies of Richmond*, p. 218.

In her journal, Mrs. Davis wrote of Christmas in 1864, excerpts from which follow:

Christmas season was ushered in under the thickest clouds; everyone felt the cataclysm which impended, but the rosy, expectant faces of our little children were a constant reminder that self-sacrifice must be the personal offering of each mother of the family. How to satisfy the children that nothing better could be done than the little makeshifts attainable in the Confederacy was the problem of the older members of each household. There were no currants, raisins or other ingredients to fill the old Virginia recipe for mince pie, and the children considered that at least a slice of the much-coveted dainty was their right....

...On Christmas morning the children awoke early and came in to see their toys....

After breakfast, at which all the family, great and small, were present, came the walk to St. Paul's Church....

We went home to find that General Lee had called in our absence and many other people. General Lee had left word that he had received a barrel of sweet potatoes for us, which had been sent to him by mistake. He did not discover the mistake until he had taken his share (a dishful) and given the rest to the soldiers. We wished it had been much more for them and him.

The night closed with a "starvation" party, where there were no refreshments, at a neighboring house. The rooms lighted as well as practicable, some one willing to play dance music on the piano and plenty of young men and girls comprised the entertainment....

So, in the interchange of courtesies and charities of life, to which we could not add its comforts and pleasures, passed....Christmas in the Confederate mansion.

Source: Jones, *Ladies of Richmond,* pp. 247-253.

Myrta Avary

Myrta Avary was a middle class woman from Virginia married to an officer in the Confederate cavalry. She wrote her memoirs, A Virginia Girl in the Civil War, *published posthumously in 1903, under the pseudonym of "Nellie Grey." In her book, Myrta Avary wrote as follows:*

I joined mother at the [hotel] Arlington, prepared to make a joke of hardships and wring every possible drop of pleasure out of a winter in Richmond, varied, as I fondly imagined, by frequent if brief visits from [husband] Dan.

The Arlington was kept on something like the European plan, not from choice of landlady or guests but from grim necessity. Feeding a household of people was too arduous and uncertain an undertaking in those days for a woman to assume. Mrs. Fry before our arrival had informed her boarders that they could continue to rent their rooms from her, but that they must provide their own meals. We paid her $25 a month for our room—the price of a house in good times and in good money. During my absence...mother, to reduce expenses, had rented half of her room and bed to Delia McArthur, of Petersburg. I now rented a little bed from Mrs. Fry for myself, and set it up in the same room.

We had become so poor and had so little to cook that we did most of our cooking ourselves over the grate, each woman often cooking her own rations. There was an old Negress living in the back yard who cooked for any or all of us when we had something that could not be prepared by ourselves over the grate. Sometimes we got hold of a roast, or we would buy two quarts of flour, a little dab of lard, and a few pinches of salt and treat ourselves to a loaf of bread, which the old Negress cooked for us, charging ten dollars for the baking. But as a rule the grate was all sufficient. We boiled rice or dried apples or beans or peas in our stew-pan, and we had a frying-pan if there was anything to fry....

Sometimes we all put what we had together and ate in company.... Sometimes we would all get so hungry that we would put together all the money we could rake and scrape and buy a bit of roast or something else substantial and have a feast....

...Dan sent me provisions by the quantity when he could get any and get them through to me....The bags of peas, rice, and potatoes were disposed around the room, and around the hearth were arranged our pots, pans, kettles, and cooking utensils generally. When we bought wood, that was put under the beds....

And we had company! Certainly we seemed to have demonstrated the truth of the adage, "Ole

Virginny never tire." We had company, and we had company to eat with us, and enjoyed it.

Sometimes our guests were boys from camp who dropped in and took stewed apples or boiled peas, as the case might be. If we were particularly fortunate we offered a cup of tea sweetened with sugar. The soldier who dropped in always got a part—and the best part—of what we had. If things were scant we had smiles to make up for the lack of our larder, and to hide its bareness.

How we were pinched that winter! how often we were hungry! and how anxious and miserable we were! And yet what fun we had! The boys laughed at our crowded room and we laughed with them....

We devised many small ways for making a little money. We knit gloves and socks and sold them, and Miss Beth Sampson had some old pieces of ante-bellum silk that she made into neckties and sold for what she could get....

For hungry and shabby as we were, crowded into our one room with bags of rice and peas, firkins of butter, a ton of coal, a small wood-pile, cooking utensils, and all of our personal property, we were not in despair. Our faith in Lee and his ragged, freezing, starving army amounted to a superstition. We cooked our rice and peas and dried apples, and hoped and prayed. By this time our bags took up little room.

We had had a bag of potatoes, but it was nearly empty. There were only a few handfuls of dried apples left—and I must say that even in the face of starvation I was glad of that!—and there was a very small quantity of rice in our larder. We had more peas than anything else....

There were hunger and nakedness and death and pestilence and fire and sword everywhere, and we, fugitives from shot and shell, knew it well, but, somehow, we laughed and sang and played on the piano—and never believed in actual defeat and subjugation....

Source: Jones, *Ladies of Richmond*, pp. 258-262.

Maria Lydig Daly

Northerner Maria Lydig Daly of New York was an upper class woman who kept a detailed diary of her Civil War experiences, excerpts from which follow:

June 11,1862—...It seems to me that the Southern women are turned into furies. The truth is that the South is jealous of the North, and hates us for our wealth and enlightenment....

February 13, 1863—It is strange to see how apathetic our people are about the war. This last fortnight has been almost like a Saturnalia, and the celebrations will finish on Tuesday with a masquerade ball at Mr. Belmont's....Last evening we went to Judge Bell's; the day before to a musical matinee at Mrs. James Brooks'; Tuesday to a grand entertainment at Mr. Francis Cutting's on the occasion of his son's marriage. The beautiful bride and her eight pretty bridesmaids were very imposing with their long, white veils....

...The women dress as extravagantly as ever, and the supper and dinner parties are far more numerous than they have been for several winters....

[Note: The federal government adopted a military draft system in July of 1863. However, a man could hire a substitute for himself for $300, which was a large amount of money at that time. The Draft Act obviously favored the rich over the poor. There was much discontent among the lower classes who resented being forced to serve in the military. They also disliked the free blacks who competed with them for low-paying jobs.]

July 14, 1863—The draft began on Saturday, the twelfth, very foolishly ordered by the government, who supposed that these Union victories would make the people willing to submit....[B]y Monday morning there were large crowds assembled to resist the draft. All day yesterday there were dreadful scenes enacted in the city. The police were successfully opposed; many were killed, many houses were gutted and burned: the colored asylum was burned and all the furniture was carried off by *women:* Negroes were hung in the streets! All last night the fire-bells rang, but at last, in God's good mercy, the rain came down in torrents and scattered the crowds, giving the city authorities time to organize. Today bodies of police and military patrolled the city to prevent any assembly of rioters....I did not wonder at the spirit in which the poor resented the three-hundred-dollar clause....The principal cause of discontent was the provision that by paying three hundred dollars any man could avoid serving if drafted, thus obliging all who could not beg, borrow, or steal this sum to go to the war. This is exceedingly unjust....

April 5, 1865—Richmond is ours! Lee is retreating!...The streets are brilliant with flags. On Saturday when the news came, there was an impromptu meeting in Wall Street. All business adjourned, a few speeches, and then the multitude sang....When I got the extra containing the great news, the tears rushed to my eyes, my heart to my throat. I could not speak. A few days more, and God be praised, it would seem as though this great trouble will be past. There will be a day of thanksgiving appointed and peace will descend upon the land. May God's blessing come with it and make us less a money-loving, selfish, and self-sufficient people, purified by this great trial....

Source: Harold Earl Hammond, ed., *Diary of a Union Lady, 1861-1865* (New York: Funk & Wagnalls Company, Inc., 1962), pp. 143, 218-219, 246, 248, 348-9.

Mary Boykin Chesnut

Mary Boykin Miller Chesnut (1823-1886) was raised in prosperity in South Carolina. After the Civil War, Mary Chesnut prepared a manuscript based upon diaries she kept during the wartime years, and the resulting book was published posthumously. Excerpts from that book and also one from her diary follow:

March 4th [1861]—...So I have seen a negro woman sold upon the block at auction. I was walking. The woman on the block overtopped the crowd. I felt faint, seasick. The creature looked so like my good little Nancy. She was a bright mulatto, with a pleasant face. She was magnificently gotten up in silks and satins. She seemed delighted with it all, sometimes ogling the bidders, sometimes looking quite coy and modest; but her mouth never relaxed from its expanded grin of excitement. I daresay the poor thing knew who would buy her. My very soul sickened. It was too dreadful. I tried to reason. "You know how women sell themselves and are sold in marriage, from queens downwards, eh? You know what the Bible says about slavery and marriage. Poor women, poor slaves....

Source: Mary Boykin Chesnut, *A Diary from Dixie* (Cambridge: Harvard University Press, 1980), pp. 10-11.

A similar excerpt from her diary for March 4, 1861 reads as follows:

I saw today a sale of Negroes—Mulatto women in *silk dresses*—one girl was on the stand. Nice looking—like my Nancy—she looked as coy & pleased at the bidder. South Carolina slave holder as I am my very soul sickened—it is too dreadful. I tried to reason—this is not worse than the willing sale most women make of themselves in marriage—nor can the consequences be worse. The Bible authorizes marriage & slavery—poor women! poor slaves!

Source: C. Vann Woodward and Elisabeth Muhlenfeld, *The Private Mary Chesnut: The Unpublished Civil War Diaries* (New York: Oxford University Press, 1984), p. 21.

March 14th [1861]—...We separated from the North because of incompatibility of temper. We are divorced, North and South, because we have hated each other so. If we could only separate politely, and not have a horrid fight for divorce....

I wonder if it be a sin to think slavery a curse to any land. Men and women are punished when their masters and mistresses are brutes, not when they do wrong....God forgive us, but ours is a monstrous system, a wrong and an iniquity!....

July 8th [1862]—...Our table talk today: this war was undertaken by us to shake off the yoke of foreign invaders, so we consider our cause righteous. The

Yankees, since the war began, have discovered it is to free the slaves they are fighting, so their cause is noble. They also expect to make the war pay. Yankees do not undertake anything that does not pay. They think we belong to them. We have been good milk cows, milked by the tariff—or skimmed. We let them have all of our hard earnings. We bore the ban of slavery; they got the money. Cotton pays everybody who handles it, sells it, manufactures it; but it rarely pays the men who make it. Second-hand, the Yankees received the wages of slavery. They grew rich; we grew poor. The receiver of stolen goods is as bad as the thief. That applies to us too. We received the savages they stole from Africa and brought to us in their slave ships....

[Late 1862-1863]—...At Kingsville [South Carolina] on my way to Camden, I caught a glimpse of Longstreet's corps going past. God bless the gallant fellows; not one man intoxicated, not one rude word did I hear. It was a strange sight. What seemed miles of platform cars, and soldiers rolled in their blankets lying in rows with their heads all covered, fast asleep. In their grey blankets packed in regular order, they looked like swathed mummies....

A feeling of awful depression laid hold of me. All these fine fellows going to kill or be killed, but why?...

Source: Chesnut, pp. 20-21, 265, 308.

Former Slaves Remember

*Between 1934 and 1941, the Federal Writers' Project,
part of the Works Progress Administration, conducted
interviews with some of the few thousand remaining
individuals who had been born into and had experienced
slavery. Excerpts from some of those interviews follow:*

MARY REYNOLDS

Slavery was the worst days that was ever seed in
the world. They was things past tellin', but I got the
scars on my old body to show to this day. I seed worse
than what happened to me....

When a nigger died, they let his folks come out
the fields to see him afore he died. They buried him the
same day—take a big plank and bus it with a ax in the
middle 'nuf to bend it back, and put the dead nigger in
betwixt it. They'd cart him down to the graveyard on
the place and not bury him deep nuf that buzzards
wouldn't come circlin' round. Niggers mourns now,
but in them days they wasn't no time for mournin'....

Source: James Mellon, ed., *Bullwhip Days: The Slaves Remember*
(New York: Weidenfeld & Nicolson, 1988), p. 18.

MARY FERGUSON

'Bout de middle of de evening', up rid my young
marster on his hoss, an' up driv' two strange white

mens in a buggy. Dey hitch deir hosses an' come in de house, which skeered me. Den, one o' de strangers said, "Git yo' clothers, Mary. We has bought yo' from Mr. Shorter." I c'menced cryin' an beggin' Mr. Shorter not to let 'em take me away. But he said, "Yes, Mary, I has sole yer, an' yer must go wid 'em."

Den, dose strange mens, whose names I ain't never knowed, tuk me an' put me in de buggy an driv' off wid me, me hollerin' at de top o' my voice an' callin' my ma. Den, dem speculataws begin to sing loud, jes' to drown out my hollerin'.

Us passed de very fiel' whar Paw an' all my folks wuz wukkin', an' I calt out as loud as I could an' as long as I could see 'em, "Good-bye, Ma! Good-bye Ma!" But she never heard me. Naw sah, dem white mens wuz singin' so loud, Ma couldn' hear me. An' she couldn' see me, 'cause dey had me pushed down out o' sight on de flo' o' de buggy.

I ain't never seed nor heard tell o' my ma an' paw, an' brothers, an' sisters, from dat day to dis.

Source: Mellon, p. 293.

KATIE ROWE

Before Old Master died he sold off a whole lot of hosses and cattle and some niggers, too. He had de sales on de plantation, and white men from around dar come to bid, and some traders come. He had a big stump whar he made de niggers stand while dey was being sold, and de men and boys had to strip off to de waist to show dey muscle and iffen dey had any scars or hurt places, but de women and gals didn't have to strip to de waist.

De white men come up and look in de slave's mouth jest lak he was a mule or a hoss....

I seen chillun sold off and de mammy not sold, and sometimes de mammy sold and a little baby kept on de place and give to another woman to raise. Dem white folks didn't care nothing 'bout how de slaves grieved when dey tore up a family.

Old Man Saunders was de hardest overseer of anybody. He would git mad and give a whipping some time, and de slave wouldn't even know what it was about....

I never forget de day we was set free.

Dat morning we all go to de cotton field early, and den a house nigger come out from Old Mistress on a hoss and say she want de overseer to come into town, and he leave and go in. After awhile, de old horn blow up at de overseer's house, and we all stop and listen, 'cause it de wrong time of day for de horn. We start chopping again, and dar go de horn again.

De lead row nigger holler, "Hold up!" And we all stop again. "We better go on in. Dat our horn," he holler at de head nigger, and de head nigger think so, too, but he say he afraid we catch de Debil from de overseer iffen we quit widout him dar, and de lead row man say maybe de overseer back from town and blowing de horn hisself, so we line up and go in....

Setting on de gallery in a hide-bottom chair was a man we never see before. He had on a big broad black hat lak de Yankees wore, but it didn't have no yaller string on it lak most de Yankees had, and he was in store clothes dat wasn't homespun or jeans, and dey was black. His hair was plumb gray and so was his beard, and it come way down here on his chest, but he didn't look lak he was very old, 'cause his face was kind of fleshy and healthy looking. I think we all been sold off in a bunch, and I notice some kind of smiling, and I think they sho' glad of it.

De man say, "You darkies know what day dis is?" He talk kind, and smile.

We all don't know, of course, and we jest stand dar and grin. Pretty soon he ask again and de head man say, "No, we don't know."

"Well dis de fourth day of June, and dis is 1865, and I want you all to 'member de date, 'cause you allus going 'member de day. Today you is free, jest lak I is, and Mr. Saunders and your mistress and all us white people," de man say.

"I come to tell you," he say, "and I wants to be sho' you all understand, 'cause you don't have to git up and go by de horn no more. You is your own bosses now, and you don't have to have no passes to go and come...."

"I wants to bless you and hope you always is happy, and tell you you got all de right dat any white people got," de man say, and den he git on his hoss and ride off....

Lots of old people lak me say dat dey was happy in slavery, and dat dey had de worst tribulations after freedom, but I knows dey didn't have no white master and overseer lak we all had on our place. Dey both dead now, and dey no use talking 'bout de dead, but I know I been gone long ago iffen dat white man Saunders didn't lose his hold on me.

It was de fourth day of June in 1865 I begins to live, and I gwine take de picture of dat old man in de big black hat and long whiskers, setting on de gallery and talking kind to us, clean into my grave wid me.

Source: Mellon, pp. 28-32.

CPSIA information can be obtained at www.ICGtesting.com
Printed in the USA
BVOW011213240612

293445BV00002B/2/P